MONTHLY *Planner* 2017

SPEEDY
PUBLISHING

Speedy Publishing LLC
40 E. Main St. #1156
Newark, DE 19711

www.SpeedyPublishing.Com

Copyright 2014

All Rights reserved. No part of this book may be reproduced or used in any way or form or by any means whether electronic or mechanical, this means that you cannot record or photocopy any material ideas or tips that are provided in this book.

2017 HOLIDAYS

JANUARY

Last Day of Chanukah (Jewish)	January 1
New Year's Day	January 1
New Year's Day (Observed)	January 2
Orthodox Christmas Day	January 7
Orthodox New Year	January 14
Martin Luther King, Jr. Day (US)	January 16
Civil Rights Day (US)	January 16
Inauguration Day (US)	January 20
Chinese New Year's Eve	January 27
First Day of Spring Festival (Chinese)	January 28

FEBRUARY

Groundhog Day (US)	February 2
Last Day of Spring Festival (Chinese)	February 2
Tu B'Shevat (Arbor Day) (Jewish)	February 11
Valentine's Day	February 14
National Flag of Canada Day	February 15
Presidents' Day (US)	February 20
Maha Shivaratri (Hindu)	February 24
Mardi Gras (US)	February 28

MARCH

Ash Wednesday (Christian)	March 1
Read Across America Day (US)	March 2
Employee Appreciation Day (US)	March 3
International Women's Day	March 8
Holi (Hindu)	March 12
Purim (Jewish)	March 12
Daylight Saving Time	March 12
Saint Patrick's Day (US)	March 17
March Equinox	March 20

APRIL

April Fools' Day	April 1
First Day of Ching Ming Festival (Chinese)	April 2
Last Day of Ching Ming Festival (Chinese)	April 4
Palm Sunday (Christian)	April 9
First Day of Passover (Jewish)	April 11
Good Friday (Christian)	April 14
Holy Saturday (Christian)	April 15
Easter (Christian)	April 16
Last Day of Passover (Jewish)	April 18
Tax Day (US)	April 18
Earth Day	April 22
Yom HaShoah (Jewish)	April 24
Isra and Mi'raj (Muslim)	April 24

MAY

Yom HaAtzmaut (Jewish)	May 2
Cinco de Mayo	May 5
Lag B'Omer (Jewish)	May 14
Mother's Day	May 14
Ramadan Begins (Muslim)	May 27
First Day of Dragon Boat Festival (Chinese)	May 28
Memorial Day (US)	May 29
Last Day of Dragon Boat Festival (Chinese)	May 30
Shavuotj (Muslim)	May 31

JUNE

Flag Day (US)	June 14
Father's Day	June 18
Laylat al-Qadr (Night of Destiny) (Muslim)	June 21
June Solstice	June 21
Eid-al-Fitr (Muslim)	June 26

JULY

Canada Day (Canada)	July 1
Canada Day (Observed) (Canada)	July 3
Independence Day (US)	July 4
Parents' Day (US)	July 23

AUGUST

Tisha B'Av (Jewish)	August 1
Heritage Day in Alberta (Canada)	August 7
Raksha Bandhan (Hindu)	August 7
Gold Cup Parade (Canada)	August 18
Statehood Day in Hawaii (US)	August 18
Discovery Day (Canada)	August 21
Women's Equality Day (US)	August 26

SEPTEMBER

Eid-al-Adha (Muslim)	September 2
Labor Day (US & Canada)	September 4
Patriot Day (US)	September 11
Constitution Day and Citizenship Day (US)	September 17
Constitution Day and Citizenship Day (US) (Observed)	September 18
Navaratri (Hindu)	September 20
Rosh Hashana (Jewish)	September 21
Muharram/Islamic New Year (Muslim)	September 22
Setember Equinox	September 22
Native Americans' Day (US)	September 22
Yom Kippur (Jewish)	September 30
Dussehra (Hindu)	September 30

OCTOBER

First Day of Sukkot (Jewish)	October 5
Columbus Day (US)	October 9
Thanksgiving Day (Canada)	October 9
Last Day of Sukkot (Jewish)	October 11
Shmini Atzeret (Jewish)	October 12
Simchat Torah (Jewish)	October 13
Diwali/Deepavali (Hindu)	October 19
Halloween (US & Canada)	October 31

NOVEMBER

Daylight Saving Time End	November 5
Veterans Day (Observed) (US)	November 10
Veterans Day (US)	November 11
Remembrance Day (Canada)	November 11
Thanksgiving (US)	November 23

DECEMBER

Prophet's Birthday (Muslim)	December 1
First Day of Hanukkah (Jewish)	December 13
Last Day of Hanukkah (Jewish)	December 20
December Solstice	December 21
Christmas Day	December 25
Boxing Day	December 26
Kwanzaa	December 26
New Years' Eve	December 31

IMPORTANT DATES

JANUARY	JULY
FEBRUARY	AUGUST
MARCH	SEPTEMBER
APRIL	OCTOBER
MAY	NOVEMBER
JUNE	DECEMBER

JANUARY

SUNDAY	MONDAY	TUESDAY	WEDNESDAY
1	2	3	4
8	9	10	11
15	16	17	18
22	23	24	25
29	30	31	

THURSDAY	FRIDAY	SATURDAY
5	6	7
12	13	14
19	20	21
26	27	28

THINGS TO DO THIS MONTH

TODAY OR ELSE	SOONER OR LATER
●	●
●	●
●	●
●	●
●	●
●	●
●	●
●	●
●	●
●	●

TO BE DONE IN THE MORNING/s	TO BE DONE IN THE EVENING/s
●	●
●	●
●	●
●	●
●	●
●	●
●	●
●	●
●	●
●	●

NOTES

FEBRUARY

SUNDAY	MONDAY	TUESDAY	WEDNESDAY
			1
5	6	7	8
12	13	14	15
19	20	21	22
26	27	28	

THURSDAY	FRIDAY	SATURDAY
2	3	4
9	10	11
16	17	18
23	24	25

THINGS TO DO THIS MONTH

TODAY OR ELSE	SOONER OR LATER
●	●
●	●
●	●
●	●
●	●
●	●
●	●
●	●
●	●
●	●

TO BE DONE IN THE MORNING/s	TO BE DONE IN THE EVENING/s
●	●
●	●
●	●
●	●
●	●
●	●
●	●
●	●
●	●
●	●

NOTES

MARCH

SUNDAY	MONDAY	TUESDAY	WEDNESDAY
			1
5	6	7	8
12	13	14	15
19	20	21	22
26	27	28	29

THURSDAY	FRIDAY	SATURDAY
2	3	4
9	10	11
16	17	18
23	24	25
30	31	

THINGS TO DO THIS MONTH

TODAY OR ELSE	SOONER OR LATER
●	●
●	●
●	●
●	●
●	●
●	●
●	●
●	●
●	●
●	●

TO BE DONE IN THE MORNING/s	TO BE DONE IN THE EVENING/s
●	●
●	●
●	●
●	●
●	●
●	●
●	●
●	●
●	●
●	●

NOTES

APRIL

SUNDAY	MONDAY	TUESDAY	WEDNESDAY
2	3	4	5
9	10	11	12
16	17	18	19
23/30	24	25	26

2017

THURSDAY	FRIDAY	SATURDAY
		1
6	7	8
13	14	15
20	21	22
27	28	29

THINGS TO DO THIS MONTH

TODAY OR ELSE	SOONER OR LATER

TO BE DONE IN THE MORNING/s	TO BE DONE IN THE EVENING/s

NOTES

MAY

SUNDAY	MONDAY	TUESDAY	WEDNESDAY
	1	2	3
7	8	9	10
14	15	16	17
21	22	23	24
28	29	30	31

THURSDAY	FRIDAY	SATURDAY
4	5	6
11	12	13
18	19	20
25	26	27

THINGS TO DO THIS MONTH

TODAY OR ELSE
●
●
●
●
●
●
●
●
●
●

SOONER OR LATER
●
●
●
●
●
●
●
●
●
●

TO BE DONE IN THE MORNING/s
●
●
●
●
●
●
●
●
●
●

TO BE DONE IN THE EVENING/s
●
●
●
●
●
●
●
●
●
●

NOTES

JUNE

SUNDAY	MONDAY	TUESDAY	WEDNESDAY
4	5	6	7
11	12	13	14
18	19	20	21
25	26	27	28

THURSDAY	FRIDAY	SATURDAY
1	2	3
8	9	10
15	16	17
22	23	24
29	30	

THINGS TO DO THIS MONTH

TODAY OR ELSE	SOONER OR LATER
●	●
●	●
●	●
●	●
●	●
●	●
●	●
●	●
●	●
●	●

TO BE DONE IN THE MORNING/s	TO BE DONE IN THE EVENING/s
●	●
●	●
●	●
●	●
●	●
●	●
●	●
●	●
●	●
●	●

NOTES

JULY

SUNDAY	MONDAY	TUESDAY	WEDNESDAY
2	3	4	5
9	10	11	12
16	17	18	19
23/30	24/31	25	26

THURSDAY	FRIDAY	SATURDAY
		1
6	7	8
13	14	15
20	21	22
27	28	29

THINGS TO DO THIS MONTH

TODAY OR ELSE	SOONER OR LATER
•	•
•	•
•	•
•	•
•	•
•	•
•	•
•	•
•	•
•	•

TO BE DONE IN THE MORNING/s	TO BE DONE IN THE EVENING/s
•	•
•	•
•	•
•	•
•	•
•	•
•	•
•	•
•	•
•	•

NOTES

AUGUST

SUNDAY	MONDAY	TUESDAY	WEDNESDAY
		1	2
6	7	8	9
13	14	15	16
20	21	22	23
27	28	29	30

THURSDAY	FRIDAY	SATURDAY
3	4	5
10	11	12
17	18	19
24	25	26
31		

THINGS TO DO THIS MONTH

TODAY OR ELSE

-
-
-
-
-
-
-
-
-
-

SOONER OR LATER

-
-
-
-
-
-
-
-
-
-

TO BE DONE IN THE MORNING/s

-
-
-
-
-
-
-
-
-
-

TO BE DONE IN THE EVENING/s

-
-
-
-
-
-
-
-
-
-

NOTES

SEPTEMBER

SUNDAY	MONDAY	TUESDAY	WEDNESDAY
3	4	5	6
10	11	12	13
17	18	19	20
24	25	26	27

2017

THURSDAY	FRIDAY	SATURDAY
	1	2
7	8	9
14	15	16
21	22	23
28	29	30

THINGS TO DO THIS MONTH

TODAY OR ELSE
●
●
●
●
●
●
●
●
●
●

SOONER OR LATER
●
●
●
●
●
●
●
●
●
●

TO BE DONE IN THE MORNING/s
●
●
●
●
●
●
●
●
●
●

TO BE DONE IN THE EVENING/s
●
●
●
●
●
●
●
●
●
●

NOTES

OCTOBER

SUNDAY	MONDAY	TUESDAY	WEDNESDAY
1	2	3	4
8	9	10	11
15	16	17	18
22	23	24	25
29	30	31	

THURSDAY	FRIDAY	SATURDAY
5	6	7
12	13	14
19	20	21
26	27	28

THINGS TO DO THIS MONTH

TODAY OR ELSE	SOONER OR LATER
●	●
●	●
●	●
●	●
●	●
●	●
●	●
●	●
●	●
●	●

TO BE DONE IN THE MORNING/s	TO BE DONE IN THE EVENING/s
●	●
●	●
●	●
●	●
●	●
●	●
●	●
●	●
●	●
●	●

NOTES

NOVEMBER

SUNDAY	MONDAY	TUESDAY	WEDNESDAY
			1
5	6	7	8
12	13	14	15
19	20	21	22
26	27	28	29

THURSDAY	FRIDAY	SATURDAY
2	3	4
9	10	11
16	17	18
23	24	25
30		

THINGS TO DO THIS MONTH

TODAY OR ELSE	SOONER OR LATER
•	•
•	•
•	•
•	•
•	•
•	•
•	•
•	•
•	•
•	•

TO BE DONE IN THE MORNING/s	TO BE DONE IN THE EVENING/s
•	•
•	•
•	•
•	•
•	•
•	•
•	•
•	•
•	•
•	•

NOTES

DECEMBER

SUNDAY	MONDAY	TUESDAY	WEDNESDAY
3	4	5	6
10	11	12	13
17	18	19	20
24/31	25	26	27

THURSDAY	FRIDAY	SATURDAY
	1	2
7	8	9
14	15	16
21	22	23
28	29	30

THINGS TO DO THIS MONTH

TODAY OR ELSE	SOONER OR LATER
●	●
●	●
●	●
●	●
●	●
●	●
●	●
●	●
●	●
●	●

TO BE DONE IN THE MORNING/s	TO BE DONE IN THE EVENING/s
●	●
●	●
●	●
●	●
●	●
●	●
●	●
●	●
●	●
●	●

NOTES

www.ingramcontent.com/pod-product-compliance
Lightning Source LLC
Chambersburg PA
CBHW081238130726
47997CB00009B/2912